What Would You Do?

THE BATTLE OF GETTYSBURG

Would You Lead the Fight?

Elaine Landau

Enslow Elementary

an imprint of

 **Enslow Publishers, Inc.**

40 Industrial Road
Box 398
Berkeley Heights, NJ 07922
USA

http://www.enslow.com

Enslow Elementary, an imprint of Enslow Publishers, Inc.

Enslow Elementary® is a registered trademark of Enslow Publishers, Inc.

Library of Congress Cataloging-in-Publication Data

Landau, Elaine.
  The Battle of Gettysburg : would you lead the fight? / Elaine Landau.
    p. cm. — (What would you do?)
  Summary: "Examines the Battle of Gettysburg, including the important military leaders, battle
    strategy, and the lasting impact this battle had on the Civil War and American history"—
    Provided by publisher.
  Includes index.
  ISBN-13: 978-0-7660-2903-3
  ISBN-10: 0-7660-2903-4
  1. Gettysburg, Battle of, Gettysburg, Pa., 1863—Juvenile literature. I. Title.
  E475.53.L27 2008
  973.7'349—dc22

                              2007041842

Printed in the United States of America

10 9 8 7 6 5 4 3 2 1

To Our Readers:
We have done our best to make sure all Internet Addresses in this book were active and appropriate
when we went to press. However, the author and the publisher have no control over and assume no
liability for the material available on those Internet sites or on other Web sites they may link to. Any
comments or suggestions can be sent by e-mail to comments@enslow.com or to the address on the
back cover.

♻ Enslow Publishers, Inc., is committed to printing our books on recycled paper. The paper in
every book contains 10% to 30% post-consumer waste (PCW). The cover board on the outside
of each book contains 100% PCW. Our goal is to do our part to help young people and the
environment too!

Every effort has been made to locate all copyright holders of material used in this book. If any errors
or omissions have occurred, corrections will be made in future editions of this book.

Illustration Credits: The Bridgeman Art Library, p. 17; © Classic Image/Alamy, p. 36; Clipart.com,
pp. 18 (insets), 26 (inset), 35 (inset); Enslow Publishers, Inc., pp. 18 (map), 26 (map), 35 (map);
© Geoffrey Kuchera, Shutterstock.com, p. 28; The Granger Collection, New York, pp. 12, 24, 31, 37,
39; Kevin Schafer/Alamy, p. 23; Library of Congress, pp. 4, 5, 6, 8, 9, 10, 11, 14, 15, 19, 20, 25, 27, 30,
32, 43; National Archives and Records Administration, p. 40; National Park Service, pp. 1, 38, 44;
© North Wind/North Wind Picture Archives—All rights reserved, p. 42; © Richard Gunion,
iStockphoto.com, p. 29.

Cover Illustration: Library of Congress.

CONTENTS

The Battle of Gettysburg was one of the most important battles fought during the American Civil War.

A Nation Torn Apart by War

In the late 1850s, differences between the Northerners and Southerners were dividing the United States.

In the North, there were businesses and factories everywhere. Yet in the South, people grew crops on large farms called **plantations**.

Southerners claimed they needed slaves to work their plantations. However, many in the North were against slavery. They did not want to see slavery spread to new areas as the country grew.

Northerners and Southerners also disagreed on how the country should be run. Most Southerners favored states' rights. They wanted the states to have more power.

President Abraham Lincoln hoped to keep the southern states from breaking away from the Union.

Gettysburg is in Pennsylvania, a state that was in the Union during the Civil War.

Many Northerners wanted a strong federal government. The federal government could overrule state laws. It would have the final say on issues like slavery.

In 1860, Abraham Lincoln was elected president. The new president was against slavery spreading to new states. Some Southerners were sure that slavery would soon be **outlawed** throughout the nation.

Following Lincoln's election, eleven states left the Union.

They formed their own nation called the Confederate States of America, or the Confederacy.

In April 1861, Confederate, or rebel, soldiers from the South attacked Fort Sumter in Charleston Harbor, South Carolina. The Civil War had begun.

By June 1863, the war had gone on for more than two years. The North had a larger army. It was also better equipped. Yet the South had won more battles.

Lincoln knew that the South would never return to the Union willingly. He needed to defeat its army.

In early June, Lincoln learned that a Southern army was moving north. The soldiers seemed to be heading for Pennsylvania.

WHAT WOULD YOU DO?

What if you were President Lincoln?

Would you . . .

✳ **Send in all your men to stop the rebel troops on their way north? If you do, many more lives will be lost. Yet what if you do not? The war might go on longer and even more lives will be lost. Or the South might win.**

LINCOLN TAKES A RISK

Lincoln made a bold move. He sent most of the Union Army's troops to Pennsylvania.

He also made Major General George Meade the Union Army's new commanding officer. Meade had a tough task. He was to keep the rebel army away from the capital—Washington, D.C.

General Robert E. Lee was in charge of the South's army. He had sent the rebel soldiers north. Lee knew that going north was risky.

However, Union soldiers had burned much of the farmland in the South. His men needed food and supplies. Finding those in the North would be easy.

Lincoln hoped Major General Meade would lead the North to victory.

General Lee also wanted to capture Gettysburg. That would put his forces closer to Washington, D.C. Then it would be easier for them to surround the capital from there. Lee also hoped that a Union defeat in the North would prevent Lincoln from being reelected president.

Lee wanted to impress England and France as well. He hoped for them to see the South's strength. Then they might offer their support.

Robert E. Lee was the top Confederate general.

Nevertheless, Lee's officers were against his plan. They felt that there were too many things that could go wrong.

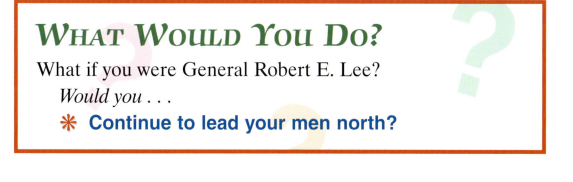

WHAT WOULD YOU DO?

What if you were General Robert E. Lee?

Would you . . .

✳ **Continue to lead your men north?**

9

GENERAL LEE MAKES A PLAN

Lee took a risk and invaded the North. He also hoped to fool the Union Army. He was counting on a special **cavalry** officer in his army to do that. That man was J. E. B. Stuart.

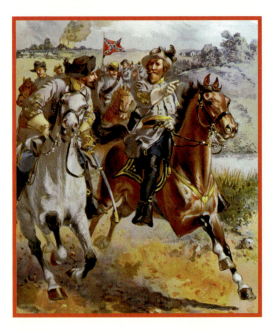

J. E. B. Stuart had led a successful raid in 1862.

Stuart was to ride with a large group of soldiers ahead of the rest of the rebel invading force. He was to draw as much attention to himself as possible. Hopefully, the Union officers would think he was leading the Confederate Army north. They would lead their Union troops to fight Stuart's force. Then they would not notice the much larger stream of men quietly entering the North at a different place.

J. E. B. Stuart was sent on a special mission.

Confederate soldiers were ready to take on the North. They were fighting for their independence from the United States.

Stuart set off with his men. He was also to keep an eye out for enemy troops. Lee needed to know where they were and how many were coming. Yet now more than two weeks had passed since Stuart left. There was still no news from him.

Stuart had come through for the rebel army in the past. Lee had even nicknamed Stuart "the eyes of the Army." Yet if Lee did not hear from Stuart soon, some Confederate officers wondered if Lee's battle plan could succeed.

WHAT WOULD YOU DO?

What if you were one of Lee's officers? You were against going north from the start. Without news from Stuart, you have no idea of where things stand.

Would you . . .

✳ **Urge General Lee to turn back? He cannot fight the enemy with so little information.**

✳ **Trust General Lee and follow orders? You know that he will get the troops through this.**

HERE'S WHAT HAPPENED:

LEE'S OFFICERS STAY LOYAL

Despite their doubts, General Lee's officers followed orders. As it turned out, J. E. B. Stuart had done well. The Union officers had no idea where the largest part of the rebel army was.

However, Stuart could not get back to Lee. The Union force had more than ninety thousand men. They filled the local roads and fields. Stuart had not found a way around them yet.

Meanwhile, the Union army was also trying to find out where the rebel army was.

Union major general John Buford and his men were the first to spot a large group of Southern troops. There were thousands of rebel soldiers just

John Buford and his men were sent to look for rebel soldiers.

14

Buford (seated) had many officers in his army whom he trusted.

three miles west of Gettysburg. The rebels were coming toward the town. Buford knew instantly that the battle would be there.

He had been ordered to find the rebels—not fight them. After all, he just had twenty-five hundred men with him. Yet he wanted to do what was best for the Union Army.

WHAT WOULD YOU DO?

What if you were Buford?

Would you . . .

* Send a few men back to get help? Then stay at the site with your men. Maybe you can hold off the rebel soldiers until help comes.

* Just go back and report what you saw? Let the highest-level officers make the decisions.

A SMALL UNION FORCE MAKES A STAND

Buford sent some men back with the news. He and his other soldiers stayed. Buford told his men to be brave.

The next morning was July 1. The rebel army attacked just after dawn.

Buford's men tried to hold off the rebel soldiers. Yet before long, they felt their position weakening. Luckily, five thousand Union soldiers arrived just in time.

Among these was the Iron Brigade. This was a well-known team of eighteen hundred Union soldiers. They were some of the best fighters in the North.

The fighting went on for hours. Cannon fire was heard for miles. Both sides were losing men. By that afternoon, almost two-thirds of the Iron Brigade was dead.

Union and Confederate soldiers battled on July 1, 1863, the first day of the Battle of Gettysburg.

DAY 1 AT GETTYSBURG: JULY 1, 1863

The Confederate soldiers attacked the Union cavalry on McPherson Ridge, west of town. By 4 P.M., the Union soldiers were overpowered, and many were captured.

Later on, five thousand more rebel soldiers arrived to join the fight. This was hard on the Union men. These rebel soldiers were fresh and eager to fight.

The tired Union forces soon weakened under fire. They were driven back to the south of town. There they positioned themselves on two hills known as Culp's Hill and **Cemetery Hill.** They also took positions on a long ridge called Cemetery Ridge.

This is Culp's Hill in Gettysburg, Pennsylvania.

General Lee was still waiting for word from J. E. B. Stuart.

General Lee remained near the battle line. His forces seemed to be winning. Still, Lee was not sure. Half his men were not there yet.

There was also still no word from J. E. B. Stuart. So Lee had no idea where the rest of the Union forces were. For all he knew, thousands could arrive within the hour.

WHAT WOULD YOU DO?

What if you were Lee?

Would you:

✴ Order all your men to attack at full force? You believe the Union soldiers are tired. You will surely win today.

✴ Be cautious? Retreat for now and start again tomorrow. By then, you will have more men. If more Union soldiers come, you will be ready for them.

GENERAL LEE WAITS

General Lee pulled back his troops. His soldiers were tired and needed rest.

However, the Union officers were not resting. The Union commander, George Meade, had arrived late that night. Meade spoke with his officers.

Some of them wanted to withdraw completely from the battle. They felt that they could not win. They had lost many men and did not want to lose more.

However, Meade did not agree. Another defeat would be very bad for the North. Besides, Meade had seventy-five thousand men heading for Gettysburg. Hopefully, they would be there before too long.

The fight could continue from the hills and ridge where the Union soldiers were now. They could move their cannons there.

A statue of Meade is in Washington, D.C.

WHAT WOULD YOU DO?

What if you were Meade?

Would you . . .

✳ **Listen to the other officers and retreat? You could save the lives of many more of your men.**

✳ **Would you stay and fight?**

MEADE STAYS TO FIGHT

Meade decided to fight. July 2, 1863, was the second day of the battle.

Meade's men formed a giant U-shaped battle line. It ran from Culp's Hill to Cemetery Ridge. The Union men dug **trenches**. They also quickly built log barriers for protection from enemy fire.

Meade's men used logs to protect themselves from rebel gunfire.

General James Longstreet led some of the Confederate forces.

DAY 2 AT GETTYSBURG: JULY 2, 1863

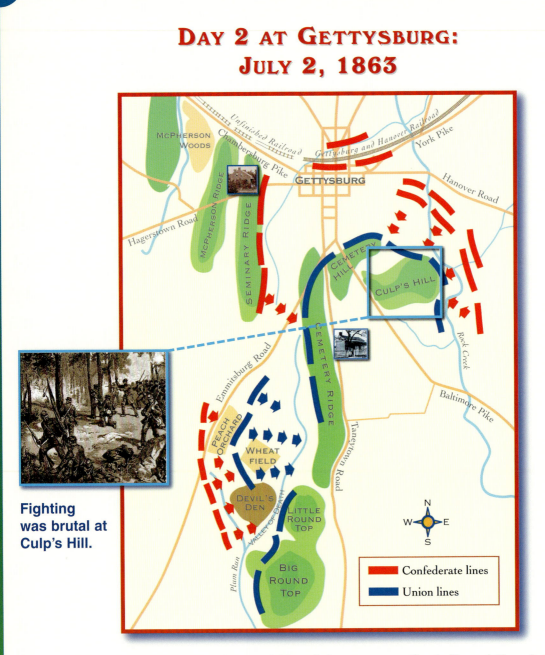

Fighting was brutal at Culp's Hill.

Confederate lines
Union lines

The Confederates attacked Meade's army on the left and the right, but the Union held on to its strong positions. The Confederates gained part of Culp's Hill, but nothing more.

Lee hoped to break through the Union line. Some of his men were to attack from the right. The rest would hit from the left.

James Longstreet was one of Lee's generals. He was to lead the attack from the left. Richard S. Ewell, another rebel general, would attack from the right.

However, Longstreet was against the plan. He did not like the idea of dividing their men that way. Longstreet wanted to circle the enemy. Then he hoped to surprise the Union soldiers by striking from the rear.

General Ewell was supposed to have his soldiers attack from the right.

Lee listened to Longstreet, but he disagreed with him. J. E. B. Stuart was not back yet. So Lee did not know how many men were behind the Union troops on the hill. He thought there might be more than his men could handle.

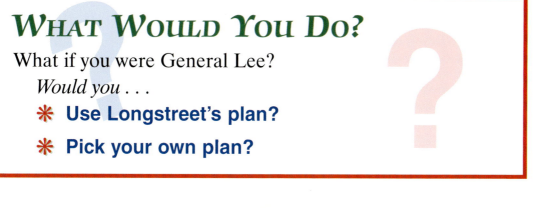

WHAT WOULD YOU DO?

What if you were General Lee?

Would you . . .

❋ **Use Longstreet's plan?**

❋ **Pick your own plan?**

LEE TAKES HIS OWN ADVICE

Lee decided to use his own plan. However, it would not be easy.

At the south end of Cemetery Ridge were two other hills known as Round Top and Little Round Top. Then at the bottom of these hills was a huge mass of rocks named Devil's Den.

Devil's Den had a lot of rocks for the Union soldiers to hide behind. This helped them avoid gunfire.

By the time the rebels attacked, the Union men were using the two hills and Devil's Den to protect themselves. The string of Union soldiers stretched out from Devil's Den to the Peach Orchard next to it.

Union forces stayed on Little Round Top because it would be hard for the Confederate soldiers to charge uphill.

Longstreet attacked from the left at about 4:00 P.M. First he hit the area near Devil's Den. The Union soldiers there fought back hard.

Next Longstreet's soldiers struck Little Round Top. Well-armed Union soldiers fought back there too.

After an hour of brutal fighting, Longstreet sent in more men. This time they attacked the Wheatfield—an area between Devil's Den and the Peach Orchard. Still another team of rebel soldiers hit the Peach Orchard as well.

The Southerners pushed back the Union soldiers at the Peach Orchard, the Wheatfield, and Devil's Den. They were

The North and South fought hard in the Peach Orchard.

General Ewell's troops charged Cemetery Hill near sunset. Edwin Forbes saw the charge and drew it. After the war, he made this painting from his drawing.

less successful at Little Round Top and Cemetery Ridge. Meade kept shifting his men to wherever they were needed.

It was nearly dark when General Ewell's men struck Culp's Hill and Cemetery Hill from the right. At the base of Cemetery Hill, they overran the Union soldiers. However, the rebel soldiers did not get much farther. By then, it was too dark to keep fighting.

The next day was July 3, 1863—the third day of battle. Lee planned to strike at the center of the Union's forces.

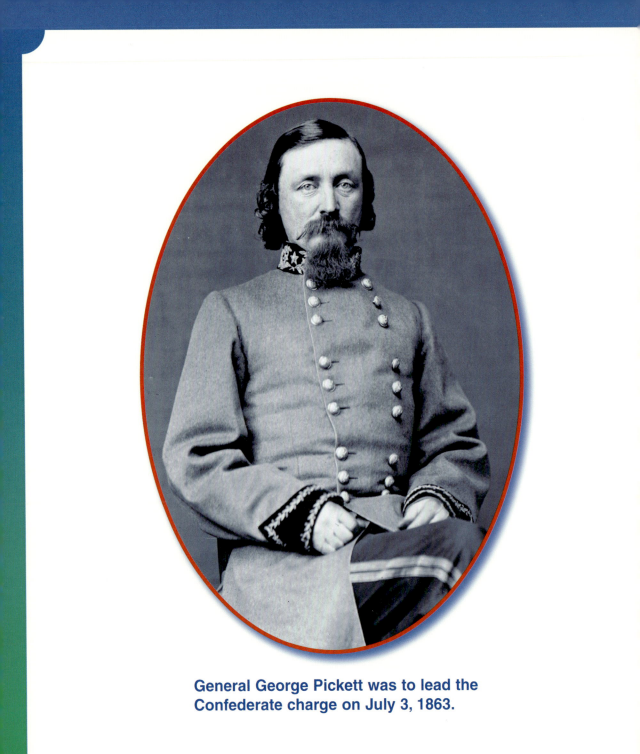

General George Pickett was to lead the Confederate charge on July 3, 1863.

Led by General George Pickett, twelve thousand rebel soldiers were to **charge** up Cemetery Ridge.

The strike would later be known as Pickett's Charge. More than 130 cannons would fire at the Union soldiers to make the charge easier for the rebel soldiers.

Also, J. E. B. Stuart had finally arrived. He and the cavalry would attack the Union troops' from the rear. A third group of rebel soldiers would strike from the right as well.

Once again, General Longstreet was against the plan. He wanted the rebel forces to withdraw. He did not feel they had enough fresh soldiers to succeed in such a large-scale attack. He feared his men would be **slaughtered**.

WHAT WOULD YOU DO?

Longstreet was Pickett's superior officer. He would have to give the order for the charge. What if you were Longstreet?

Would you . . .

* **Order the charge?**
* **Refuse to do it?**

LONGSTREET HESITATES

Longstreet did not want to order the charge. He doubted that they could defeat the Union soldiers that day. So he passed this task on to the head **artillery** officer, Colonel E. P. Alexander.

At 1:00 P.M., the rebels began firing over 130 cannons. This went on for about an hour and a half. The Union Army fired its cannons back. They hit their mark more often than the rebels.

Alexander sent word to Pickett to start the charge. However, the command had not come from Longstreet. So Pickett ignored it.

About ten minutes later, Alexander sent the command again. This time he urged Pickett to hurry. Alexander's men were running out of **ammunition**. He would barely have enough to cover Pickett's men as they charged.

Pickett looked for Longstreet on the battlefield. He found him sitting on a fence watching the cannon fire. Pickett asked: "Do you want me to charge?"

DAY 3 AT GETTYSBURG: JULY 3, 1863

The Union Cavalry

Unfinished Railroad

Chambersburg Pike

Gettysburg and Hanover Railroad

York Pike

GETTYSBURG

Hanover Road

McPHERSON RIDGE

SEMINARY RIDGE

CEMETERY HILL

CULP'S HILL

Rock Creek

Cavalry battle took place 3 miles east →

Custer's cavalry

Stuart's cavalry

CEMETERY RIDGE

Emmitsburg Road

PEACH ORCHARD

WHEAT FIELD

Taneytown Road

DEVIL'S DEN

VALLEY OF DEATH

LITTLE ROUND TOP

Plum Run

BIG ROUND TOP

N W E S

	Confederate lines
	Union lines

Pickett's Charge would be a challenge to the Confederate forces.

Finally, Longstreet (standing) ordered Pickett (on horse) to begin his charge. In reality, Longstreet was sitting on a fence, not standing up.

General Longstreet could not bring himself to answer. He simply nodded and raised his hand. Pickett began the uphill charge.

The rebel soldiers went forward in an open field. That made them easy targets for the Union soldiers' fire.

Pickett's Charge was a disaster for the Confederate Army.

Shells ripped through the rebel soldiers' bodies. Body parts flew about the field. Hundreds of men fell. The ground was soon covered with bloody **corpses**.

WHAT WOULD YOU DO?

What if you were a rebel soldier? You are at the back of the advancing group.

Would you . . .

* ✳ **Continue to charge?**
* ✳ **Run from the battlefield?**

LEE'S ATTACK FAILS

Some rebel soldiers **deserted**, or ran from, the battlefield that day. Most remained loyal and fought hard.

But Lee's attack failed. After many men had fallen, the rebel forces finally backed off. There were tears in Pickett's eyes when he left the battlefield.

As the battle grew more fierce, some rebel soldiers deserted. Most, however, stayed to fight.

Confederate soldier William Dorsey Pander was wearing this uniform when he was wounded at Gettysburg.

This surgical tent was set up at Gettysburg. A surgeon is preparing to amputate a soldier's wounded leg.

What was left of the rebel fighting force headed south with Lee. The line of **wounded** soldiers stretched for more than fourteen miles.

The loss of human life was high. More than seventy-five hundred died in battle. There were 4,637 rebel soldiers killed. The Union had 3,149 men who lost their lives as well. Thousands more from both sides were badly injured.

After the battle, hospitals were needed for the wounded. There were over twenty thousand Union and rebel soldiers needing serious care. They were treated in fields, churches, public buildings, and even people's homes.

Nevertheless, after the fighting at Gettysburg, Lincoln urged Meade to attack the rebels before they got away.

Meade was not sure this was a wise military move.

WHAT WOULD YOU DO?

Meade's men were tired after the battle at Gettysburg. They had fought hard and many were wounded. At that point, the Union troops were running out of food as well. Meade did not feel ready for another battle just yet.

What if you were Meade?

Would you . . .

✱ **Do what Lincoln wanted?**

✱ **Hold your troops back?**

THE UNION WAITS TO WIN AGAIN

Meade did what Lincoln asked. On July 4, 1863, he and his men followed Lee out of Gettysburg. It was hard to track the rebel soldiers because of a heavy rainstorm that day.

The Confederate army used the cover of a rainstorm to escape from Meade's soldiers.

General Lee's men were able to quickly get across the Potomac River. Soon they were safely in Virginia.

Meanwhile, in Gettysburg, the dead soldiers had not received proper burials. There was neither time nor money for that. Graves were simply dug all over the battlefield area.

Some who lived in Gettysburg felt that these men deserved more respect. A cemetery was planned for the fallen soldiers in Gettysburg. The opening for the cemetery was held on November 19, 1863.

That day, Lincoln gave a two-minute address in memory of the fallen soldiers. His speech became known as the Gettysburg Address. Though short, it is one of the most

Lincoln gave one of his most famous speeches at the opening of the new cemetery at Gettysburg. His speech was later called the Gettysburg Address.

famous speeches in American history. In it, Lincoln said this of the fallen soldiers: "The world will little note, nor long remember what we say here, but it can never forget what they [the soldiers] did here."

The Civil War went on for two more years. Yet the battle at Gettysburg was an important turning point.

The South never got over its losses that day. Lee's army was reduced by a third. Rebel forces were not strong enough to attack in Northern territory again. In the end, the North won the war in 1865.

The Battle of Gettysburg might have been what the North needed. Yet it came at a great human cost—many men on both sides gave their lives on those first three days in July 1863.

Today, this statue at Gettysburg honors the soldiers that fought there.

TIMELINE

1860—Abraham Lincoln is elected president.

1860–1861—Some Southern states leave the Union and form a new nation called the Confederate States of America.

1861—*April:* Confederate soldiers attack a Union fort—Fort Sumter in South Carolina; the Civil War begins.

1863—*June:* A Southern army is spotted moving North toward Pennsylvania. In late June, Lincoln makes General George Meade commander of all Union forces.

July 1: Confederate soldiers attack Gettysburg just after dawn. The Confederate troops do well that day.

July 2: The second day of the Gettysburg battle. Both sides make some gains, but lose men. By the day's end, there is no clear winner.

July 3: The Union wins the Battle of Gettysburg.

July 4: General George Meade goes after the remaining Confederate troops as they head back South. The rebels make it safely to Virginia.

November 19: The opening ceremony for a soldiers' cemetery at Gettysburg is held. Lincoln delivers the Gettysburg Address.

1865—The North wins the Civil War.

WORDS TO KNOW

ammunition—Something fired from a weapon, like a bullet or cannonball.

artillery—The part of an army that uses big guns.

cavalry—Soldiers who fight on horseback.

cemetery—A place where dead people are buried.

charge—An advance or strike by a group of soldiers in battle; can also mean to advance or strike.

corpse—A dead human body.

desert—To run away from the army.

outlawed—Made illegal.

plantations—Large farms.

rebel—A Southern soldier who fought in the Civil War.

retreat—To withdraw from a battle.

slaughtered—Killed in mass numbers.

trenches—Low, narrow ditches.

wounded—Injured or hurt.

LEARN MORE

Books

DeAngelis, Gina. *The Battle of Gettysburg: Turning Point of the Civil War.* Mankato, Minn.: Bridgestone Books, 2003.

Elish, Dan. *The Battle of Gettysburg.* Danbury, Conn.: Children's Press, 2005.

O'Hern, Kerri. *The Battle of Gettysburg.* Milwaukee, Wisc.: World Almanac Library, 2006.

Tanaka, Shelley. *A Day That Changed America: Gettysburg: The Legendary Battle and the Address That Inspired a Nation.* New York: Hyperion Books for Children, 2003.

Venezia, Mike. *Abraham Lincoln: Sixteenth President, 1861–1865.* Danbury, Conn.: Children's Press, 2005.

Internet Addresses

The Battle of Gettysburg
<www.nps.gov/gett/forkids/index.htm>
Visit this Web site to learn about Gettysburg National Military Park. Do not miss the History & Culture link for lots of great information on the battle fought there in 1863.

General Robert Edward Lee
<www.nps.gov/anti/lee_bio.htm>
Check out this Web site for great information on that famous Southern military man—Robert E. Lee. Do not miss the picture gallery link!

INDEX